Table of Content

Preface v

Your Worth is in Your Birth 7

Discovering Your Hidden Treasure 13

I Can 23

Start Where Others Stopped 31

Net Worth Is The Fruit/Self-worth Is The Root 39

About The Author.. 45

PREFACE

Who cares about self-worth as long as one makes a modest living? Well, if an unpresumptuous income is all you want out of life than an unhealthy self-esteem will ensure that modest would be your financial ceiling.

How you feel about yourself is oftentimes affiliated with how much you will achieve during your lifetime. Your self-worth is closely associated with your net worth. It is commonly known that low income wage people are oftentimes associated with low self-esteem. It may not be in all cases because people generally have to work their way up the latter. However, if a person can believe the Bible and what it says about them, it can cause the priceless gems in a person's belief system to generate, and will ultimately transmute into income potential.

Don't be blinded or closed minded to the treasures hidden in your earthen vessel. After reading this book, it will inspire you to dream everyday regardless of your personal resume. It will also teach you how to listen and learn for ways to earn. The more you learn, the more you earn. So, go ahead; squeeze the trigger of thinking bigger. Don't hesitate to initiate to show others a sample of success by example.

THE POCKET MOTIVATOR BOOK SERIES

A Proven Method of How Your Self-Worth
Can Improve Your Net Worth

SELF-WORTH
NET WORTH

The Truth that You Are More Like God then You Think.

DR. MIKEL BROWN

Self-Worth Net Worth:
A Proven Method of How Your Self-Worth Can Improve Your Net Worth

CJC PUBLISHING COMPANY

1208 Sumac Drive
El Paso, TX 79925

Copyright © 2018 by Mikel Brown. All Rights Reserved
Printed in the United States of America

ISBN: 978-1-930388-23-9

Editorial assistance for CJC Publishing Co. by Caryn Newman
Cover design by CJC Advertising Agency

All scripture references are from the King James Verison of the Bible unless otherwise noted.

No part of this publication may be reproduced, stored in a retrieval system or transmitted in any form or by any means, electronic, mechanical, photocopying, recording, scanning or otherwise, except as permitted under Sections 107 or 108 of the 1976 United States Copyright Act, without either the prior written permission of the Publisher. Request to the Publisher for permission should be addressed to the Permissions Department, CJC Publishing, 1208 Sumac Drive, El Paso, Texas 79925, 915-595-1307, fax 915-1493.

Limit of Liability/Disclaimer of Warranty: While the publisher and author have used their best efforts in preparing this book, they make no representations or warranties with respect to the accuracy or completeness of the contents of this book and specifically disclaim any implied guarantees. The advice and strategies contained herein are not suitable for every individual. You should consult with a professional as it concerns your specific situation. Neither the publisher nor author shall be liable for any outcome concerning ones marriage or common law relationship, included but not limited to special, incidental, consequential, or other damages.

YOUR WORTH IS IN YOUR BIRTH

Evaluating oneself should never involve determining one's worth.

This quote was birthed out of the ashes of despair, a failed marriage and a rapidly diminishing income. To simply bounce back seemed hopeless. How do you avoid commingling self-worth with performance, and even more, net worth? To say the least, this task is a difficult one. Now, I did not say that it was impossible! Things that are difficult are labor intensive and demand a greater focus and tenacity in order to defeat their challenges. I had to become intentional with my aim and deliberate with my attack. Despite my disappointments and frustrations, I had to some how find my target in life again.

Usually people struggle with the difficulties of maintaining thoughts concerning themselves. Most people wrestle with hidden thoughts of inferiority, inadequacies, and or the fear of not being able to measure up. Most people use their past failures as a premise for these thoughts of incompetence. They balance their failures against their qualities and for them, their qualities always lose out.

Allow me to ask you a series of questions. Who or what are you measuring yourself up against? Who or what experience can identify or is licensed to be ranked in the same lump of clay with you? I will answer these questions with an emphatic, "No one and nothing!" When you were born, the mold went out with the afterbirth (placenta) that circumscribed your life while you were in your mother's womb. Therefore, absolutely nothing can compare to you.

Nothing in creation, not even another human being is in your category. Your specific DNA and fingerprints are evidence of this, and they qualify your uniqueness. Don't make the fatal mistake of diminishing your value because of mistakes that are made. You don't throw the baby out with the dirty bath water. You may have made mistakes in your life with the choices you've made, but it does not mean that you are a mistake.

You are a creative and powerful being with intrinsic qualities that cannot be reduced or condensed. The Creator breathed the imperial quality of your creation into you; therefore, what is in the Creator, is now in you. I realize all the things that can and have happened to people on this planet can cause them to have a sense of inadequacy. I am also aware of the potential that is hidden behind or buried under the years of hurt and devastation. But not even the worse things that have occurred in your life are able to lessen who you really are. My friend, gold is still gold regardless of where you find it. Whether you discover it in the mountains or in the trash can, its worth is intrinsic value and it cannot be diminished based on the locality of its discovery.

Your worth as a person was not given to you as a result of the accolades from your parents, teachers, and coaches who were only happy when you did something right. If human worth were based on our performances, all of humanity would be worthless.

---

*You don't get what you deserve;
you get what you take.*

Your worth was in your birth! God exhaled life and you inhaled it. Consequently, no person, experience, or performance—good or bad can decrease or increase your worth.

Land and houses depreciate or appreciate based on how other equivalent homes and land are selling in the area. Can you now see how important it is to understand what is in you, so that you will not reduce your life to a mere experience? You are not a plot of land that can be negotiated or traded as though you have no significance.

Whenever people make a mistake they seldom say anything encouraging to themselves. They usually relegate their intelligence to that of a dunce by using words such as stupid, idiot, or some other demeaning term. Worthless, is how most people feel after a mistake, like a child who fails in some sporting activity; but this is only a feeling or an emotion. You may not feel worthy of what it was you were trying to accomplish, but you are worth the next attempt to take it.

You don't always get what you deserve in life, and thank God because there are some things you don't want to come to you; but you do get what you take in life. You may have to convince yourself that you deserve the things you've worked hard for and the rewards and accolades that are associated with those things. Worthiness has nothing to do with it, but faith in God and hard work does.

Christians are often recorded saying how unworthy they are of all that Christ has done for humanity at Calvary. I discovered something that I believe will actually revolutionize your whole life once you grasp its truth. Due to my next statement, some critics will have the unmitigated gall to categorize this book as religious material. When in fact, this book highlights inter-relational and personal fundamental principles to help assist the reader on developing a systematic outlook concerning him or herself.

It is very true that we as humans are unworthy of the death of God's only begotten Son, Jesus. It is also true that we can never pay for or earn what He did. Since we are undeserving, unworthy but not worthless, why did God do all of these wonderful things for us? Would you do something for someone who rejects you? It appears as if God went out on the limb for people who don't believe in Him. When God sent His only begotten Son to suffer an excruciating death on the cross for you and me, He could not measure us on merit. God had to gauge His action for humanity on worth, not worthiness. Although we were not worthy, we were yet worth it.

Too much is invested in you to allow you to live out your years relegated to a life of deficiency. God is simply protecting His investment. Life is too precious to waste and too costly to negotiate. If my statement of truth went over your head, please read it again until you catch the revelation of it. Some things are better caught than taught.

DISCOVERING YOUR HIDDEN TREASURE

Now that I'm aware of my worth, what now? Your next step is to go on a treasure hunt. Sound exciting? Well, it is invigorating to say the least. I can remember as a kid going to church on Easter. Those days were fun and innocent times. Our Sunday school teachers would hide Easter eggs, gifts, and prizes for anyone who could find the hidden eggs. Each egg discovered, would reveal a prize. This was equivalent to the treasure hunt I'm speaking of. Each time you discover something about yourself, you get a prize produced by your discovery. You begin to see how something hidden can manifest into something visible.

The treasures locked away on the inside of you, are locked away for a reason. This wealth was not haphazardly place in you. It was very intentional and deliberate. Most people search from without to find worth, but it takes character to examine within to find strength and value.

What an odd place to hide something so priceless and invaluable. People will look everywhere on God's green earth to find treasure except within themselves. You are not cheap worthless material that sparkles and shines on the surface. People who understand their value are fully aware that the shine on the outside is from an innate beauty that resonates from within. You are a wealth of treasure waiting to be explored. You alone hold the key to your treasure box. Others can tell you what they see in you, but only you can unlock the potential that others may or may not see. Do not be afraid to look inside of yourself. Go ahead and look! Tell me, what do you see? Once you view its splendor, no one will be able to tell you who he or she thinks you are.

I can recall when my second son began to discover his potential to read as a child. When he was five years old, he was reading on a second-grade level. As I was driving down the freeway one day, I noticed he would audibly read all the billboard signs. Everything he saw, he read out loud. The big words did not stop him from reading. He would break the words down phonetically until he enunciated the words correctly. A whole 'New World' had opened up

Discovering Your Hidden Treasure

to him and the potential was endless. I have never heard of treasure being found on the street corner or in the most obvious places. Usually, people who intentionally dig, search, dynamite or even break things for it, find it. These people will literally humiliate themselves, which is a small price to pay for something priceless.

How far down must you dig in order to discover your hidden treasure? Is it worth shoveling through

---
*You can file bankruptcy,
but you can never be bankrupt.*

---

the pain of a divorce, the abuse as a child, the failure in business, or the abandonment of your parents?

Do you consider your present pain a treasured possession, so much so, that you are unwilling to excavate the soil of your soul to truly determine the prize of your existence? I know how pain seems to demand more attention than what really should be focused on at the time. But considering the circumstances, pain will have to wait until I can properly pause without causing more damage to myself.

One day I was driving down the road and was suddenly hit with excruciating pain in my abdomen. It was not a heart attack, so I was able to endure the pain without dying. I was bent over with this abrupt pain in the middle of 55 mile per hour traffic. I was in the midst of a dilemma. I could either allow this pain to drive me into oncoming traffic, and risk dying, or I could endure the pain long enough to pull over and minimize my risk of injury. What was more important to me was living beyond my pain to see another day. The moral of the story is that I chose not to allow my present pain to destroy my tomorrow.

Each day you wake up, you are privileged to see a day you have never seen before. You cannot make right today the wrong mistakes you made yesterday. However, you can avoid yesterday's mistakes by recognizing them today. A sign of maturity is your ability to identify your past mistakes so you can avoid duplicating them. If you find yourself repeating the same errors, you have not learned to detect the warning signs from your experiences. In my book, "Beyond Ordinary" I mentioned that life is a series of lessons. Unfortunately, it doesn't always guarantee us a passing grade. Nonetheless, my grade is predicated on my ability to aggressively shift the gears of life into fourth gear and move beyond park.

My aim is not to impress you, but to impress upon

you the importance of discovering your worth and learning to respect it. To respect yourself, is to give the highest grade possible without comparing yourself to any person or sentencing yourself to defeat. You can file bankruptcy, but you can never be bankrupt. There is too much concealed inside of you. It is impossible to lose everything because you don't have a clue of how much treasure is stored inside of you. I do not believe that we can fully unveil all that is locked up on the inside of us.

Humans are the crowns of God's creation. Yet, some people are quick to dethrone their intrinsic destiny based upon a bad choice that was made or some unfortunate circumstance. Your money, car, career, spouse, children, house(s), land, divorce, environment, friends or any other thing, good or bad, cannot define you as a person. If these things are necessary in order for you to feel good about yourself, then your life is worth zero. These things have no real value. You can always obtain material things, but you can never repeat life. I often say that life is not a rehearsal. I often find myself repeating this phrase wherever I go, because it is easy for me to recognize the shortsightedness of people.

Self-Worth Net Worth

If you treat your day with reckless abandonment, then conflict will be the product manufactured at the end of the day. But if you respect the day that you are privileged to enjoy by pouring into it what you want produced at the end of it, you will find it waiting for you. Today is too precious for you to treat it as though it is a wastebasket. Put good things into your day and good things will spill over into your tomorrow. There is more than enough treasure stored inside of you to brighten your day and the day of others as well. You are electrifying; you are powerful. In fact, Jesus said, "You are the light of the world." Just think, the person that you see in the mirror every day has qualities that have not been identified. You have creative ability,

---
You have creative ability, which translates into power.

---

which translates into power. People like having power; many people just don't believe they have much of it. On the contrary! You are jammed-packed with authority and creative power.

What may not be apparent does not mean it does not exist. We are surrounded by invisible things, which can be transposed or inverted. I know this may sound crazy to some, but in reality, it is true. Faith is the most energizing tool given to mankind. Faith never operates alone; it is always accompanied by deeds. I exemplify my faith by what I believe so strongly to perform. My faith believes in something that does not yet exist, but my deeds transpose my faith (invisible) into actual material.

You may not be able to presently observe the hidden treasure in you, but let me assure you that I will do everything in my power to clear your nebulous

---
Learn to invest in your qualities and they will cause you to be numbered among great men.

---

view. I want to greatly inform you so you can be reformed. Call out the search party because you are about to experience the most spine tingling, eye-popping time of your life.

I wrote this book on self-worth...so you might know yours. Your power is released through your knowledge, not your ignorance. Your treasure is not in your business, bank account, investment portfolio, spouse, children, car, plane or yacht. Get ready for this powerful simple statement! You Are the Treasure! You are Your Greatest Asset. Everything about you speaks increase, money, or commodity. Does your job

Self-Worth Net Worth

pay you for just having your name on the employee roster? NO! Your employer pays you for working.

You need not one supplementary item added to you in order to be consummated.

Whatever amount of hourly wage or salary you agree to exchange your abilities for each day is exactly what you will be paid. What you agreed to get paid does not determine what your life is worth. No job can pay you what you are worth.

When you labor eight hours or more a day, you are giving of your time, energy, and mental ability. This, my friend is your life. The company you work for will never consider the wear and tear on your body, but they will consider the wear and tear on their machines. Each time you go to work, you are giving a little of your life away. As you commence to review this, your mind will start to process this information. Consequently, your career, business, and material things will begin to lose their value and "You" will begin to stand out from all of these. You can manufacture these material things anytime you like because you are the source that attracts them. Learn to invest in your qualities and they will cause you to be numbered among great men. As you unfold your worth, even your weakness can become your greatest asset. Separate "YOU" from your business, home, career and the accumulation of material things. You need not one supplementary item added to you in order to be consummated. Your production of things cannot add, multiply, or magnify who you are. You are the one who amplifies the clothes, cars, houses, and business. Clothes need a body to rest on; cars need someone to drive them; houses need people to live in them, and a business needs a mastermind and a prime mover. Therefore, make the best out of the rest of your life, because you can and you are sentenced to succeed.

There was a man in the Bible whose name was Job. He was the Prince of the East and he was very wealthy. He was not like most rich people who placed all their self-worth in what they own. Job really loved his family and he epitomized it by making prayer for his family a daily custom. One day the devil gained permission from God to test, stress, and stretch Job. The devil stole his livestock, destroyed his land and real estate, and even killed his children. To add insult to injury, the devil caused his body to break out in ugly sores. Under these circumstances, I would think that most people would break under the weight of this pressure. Job went from a wealthy Prince of the East to the pauper on the corner in just a matter of days.

How do you think you would do if you were faced with the concerns Job had to encounter? Why do you suppose that the devil's emphasis was placed on material things? I believe that one of the principles God was revealing to Job was the value of intrinsic material and the lesser value of earthly material. Through all of Job's experiences he learned that he could be stretched and not snap; bend, and not break; be knocked down, but not knocked out. While most people would experience a nervous breakdown, Job experienced a powerful breakthrough. Why? The answer is easy; he believed more in the inherent quality of his character and the God Who lived in him than all the bad things that happened to him.

I CAN

I can dismantle every frustrating thought and disarm every challenge with just two words; I CAN!

It has been said that the rational mind is a wonderful servant but a terrible master. We must control the mind instead of giving it free reign to run wild. If we do not control the mind it will team up with the mouth and the tongue, and together they can lead us into trouble.

> 2 Corinthians 10:4 (KJV) (For the weapons of our warfare [are] not carnal, but mighty through God to the pulling down of strong holds;) {through God: or, to God} 5 Casting down imaginations, and every high thing that exalteth itself against the knowledge of God, and bringing into captivity every thought to the obedience of Christ; {imaginations: or, reasonings} 6 And having in a readiness to revenge all disobedience, when your obedience is fulfilled.

Self-Worth Net Worth

One day a man was troubled because he was experiencing dizzy spells. He went from one doctor to another, but none could diagnose the problem. He began to lose weight, and stopped sleeping at night. His health continued to deteriorate so that he began to prepare for the worst. He went to a clothing store and picked out a suit, shoes, socks, and asked the store clerk for a size 15 shirt. The store clerk said, "Sir, you need between a 16-17 size shirt, but the man insisted that he wore a size 15 in the neck. Finally, in exasperation, the clerk said, "But if you wear a size fifteen you'll get dizzy spells."

The most difficult part of a person to change is their mind. A mind that is not harnessed will produce and justify failure, destroy relationships, conjure ill feelings, and rationalize the destruction of its own body. A person should never believe the tongue of a bitter and stubborn heart. I have learned that the body can change and adjust if the person is willing to change their mind. It is neither your body nor your mouth that is usually out of control; it is your mind.

Carter G. Woodson wrote a powerful paragraph about controlling a man. He said, "If you can control a man's thinking, you do not have to worry about his actions. When you determine what a man shall think, you do not have to concern yourself about what he will do. If you make a man feel that he is inferior, you do not have to compel him to accept an inferior status, for he will seek it himself. If you make a man think that he is justly an outcast; you do not have to order him to the back door. He will go without being told; and if there is no back door, his very nature will demand one."

It has been said, "Sow an action and you will reap a habit; sow a habit and you will reap a character; sow a character and you will reap a destiny." How you think determines your actions, your actions determine your habits and your habits will determine where you will end up.

Most Christians are more dedicated to dying for Christ than they are to living for Christ. If you are not willing to live for Christ, you will evade the opportunity of dying for Him. The proof of your dedication is how you choose to live for Him. Jesus spent three years of earthly ministry raising the level of thinking in those who followed Him. Everything Jesus did was His way of demonstrating to us that we can do it too.

Two weekend fishermen were in a boat fishing. One man caught three large trout and threw them back into the water. Whenever he caught a smaller fish, he would keep them. The other fisherman, puzzled by his actions asked, "Why are you throwing back the large fish and keeping the fish that are no bigger than a small sardine." "My frying pan is small." Replied the man.

This man turned down opportunities because he was restricted by the size of his frying pan. How many wealth-creating opportunities have you thrown back because you believed your capacity was limited? Generally, people are more limited by their ability to soberly and courageously believe they are capable of things than by their ability to perform them. Don't fear success because it is God's design for your life. You were created and wired for success, but during your young life you were programmed for failure.

Whenever you're stretched, your capacity is enlarged. The law of wealth and success could care

---
You can rise above and be superior to every condition through the strength that Christ gives.

---

less about who you are, what your background is, your physical deficiencies, race or gender. It bends and serves anyone who will not only accept its graces, but will apply its potential.

Romans 12:2 (NIV) Do not conform to the pattern of this world, but be transformed by the renewing of your mind. Then you will be able to test and approve what God's will is-- his good, pleasing and perfect will. 3 For by the grace given me I say to every one of you: Do not think of yourself more highly than you ought, but rather think of yourself with sober judgment, in accordance with the faith God has distributed to each of you.

People who usually wrestle with low self-esteem, do not have a good healthy God-esteem. Building your worth-value is discovering what God says about you. A handicapped man was recorded saying, "I know I'm going to make it in spite of my handicap. I will not be a prisoner of a wheel chair. I know I can make it."

There are not enough of us saying, "I Can!" A person can be at least ten times more powerful, at least ten times happier and freer and stronger than they are if they will simply change and believe two words. We can be ten times more active, more alive, more spiritual, more faithful, and more God-like if we will only say, "I Can," instead of I Can't! "I Can" is the language of God. In fact, God declares, "Is there anything too hard for Me."

> Philippians 4:13 (KJV) I can do all things through Christ which strengtheneth me.

You can rise above and be superior to every condition through the strength that Christ gives. It's not the load that breaks you down, it's the way you have been taught to carry it. An overburdened and overworked ant was carrying a piece of straw across a large slab of concrete. The straw was so long and heavy that the tiny insect staggered beneath its weight. Nonetheless, the ant was committed to completing its task. Finally, as the stress of its burden began to take its toll, the little ant was brought to a halt by a gaping crack in its path. The ant saw no way of getting across or around the deep divide. Then a thought suddenly struck. Carefully laying the straw across the gulf, the ant walked over it and safely reached the other side. The ant's heavy load had become a helpful bridge because he was committed to his task.

> Proverbs 6:6 Go to the ant, you sluggard; consider its ways and be wise! 7 It has no commander, no overseer or ruler, 8 yet it stores its provisions in summer and gathers its food at harvest. 9 How long will you lie

there, you sluggard? When will you get up from your sleep? (NIV)

Every act of Christ was a framed picture that pointed us towards our potential. In order to survive the increased attacks on our minds, from temptation to money problems, Christians need to take a whole different approach to winning in life. Through nutritional research, we've learned that the body reflects the diet it is fed. Physical stamina, resistance to disease, body size, even how long we live is all closely related to what we eat. The body is the sum of what it is fed. By the same token, the mind is the sum of what the mind is fed. Mind food is made up of the countless things that influence conscious and subconscious thoughts.

Psychiatrists say there are only two fears we are born with. One is the fear of falling and the other is the fear of loud sound. So all other fears are learned. The fear of failure is a learned behavior and so is the fear of success. These are two of the most crippling fears. Average people are rarely successful and they don't like change! Resistance to change is the natural inclination of the average person, regardless of the benefits of the change. Do you know how 10% of the people get 90% of the pie? The ten percent exercise the willingness to change and adapt; and they maintain an attitude conducive to winning. If you believe you can, then you will. See you at the top!

WHEN SELF-WORTH BECOMES NET WORTH

Let me start with a statement that will break chains off someone's mind: you will never rise above the value you place upon yourself. Money follows meaning, and meaning is rooted in worth. Self-worth is not arrogance, not pride, not performance. Self-worth is the God-breathed realization that you are priceless, even when the world tries to tag you with a clearance sticker.

The Difference Between Self-Worth and Performance-Worth

Most people confuse what they do with who they are. They believe a job title makes them valuable, or a failed relationship makes them worthless. This is the lie that keeps destinies dormant and people feeling worthless.

- Performance-worth says: "If I perform

well, then I am valuable."

- Self-worth declares: "I am valuable, therefore I perform well."

This shift sounds subtle, but it is seismic. The enemy of your soul and mind wants you to confuse the two so you'll spend your life performing for applause while dying of emptiness. But God says your worth was written before your first breath. That's why you're here today.

The Psalmist wrote: "I will praise Thee; for I am fearfully and wonderfully made" (Psalm 139:14). Notice—he praised God not for a paycheck, not for achievements, but for being.

There is a Story of Broken Glass and Priceless Diamonds:

Years ago, a young man worked at a pawn shop. He told the story of how a lady brought in a jewelry box. In it was a diamond necklace she thought was worthless costume jewelry. For decades it sat in her drawer. The pawn broker inspected it and gasped—it was a rare stone worth more than her house.

That's how people live: priceless diamonds buried

under the dust of false beliefs. They dismiss themselves as "ordinary" because others never saw their sparkle. But heaven never misjudged your worth.

Here's the truth: What you think is costume jewelry is kingdom treasure. And the moment you accept your self-worth, your life's net worth begins to multiply.

Self-Worth Determines Your Financial Ceiling

Hear this clearly: your bank account is often a reflection of your belief account. If you secretly believe you don't deserve abundance, you'll sabotage every opportunity that comes your way. You'll undersell your gifts, underprice your products, and undervalue your contribution.

Money is attracted to confidence, but confidence is born from worth. Why do millionaires invest in coaching, branding, and image? Because they know perception creates reality. If you see yourself small, life will hand you small checks. If you see yourself through God's worth, doors swing wide.

How Self-Worth Unlocks Wealth

1. **It shifts how you speak.** Words flow from identity. If you think little, you'll talk little. But when you know you're chosen, your language upgrades. Instead of saying, "I'm just trying," you declare, "I am building, I am creating, I am multiplying."

2. **It reshapes your associations.** When your worth rises, you stop tolerating toxic circles. Worthy people attract worthy relationships. Proverbs 13:20 says, "He that walketh with wise men shall be wise."

3. **It redefines what you tolerate.** Poverty, fear, and abuse cannot stay in the same house where worth is awakened. Self-worth is eviction notice to everything that diminishes destiny.

A Slight Adjustment Creates a God-Sized Life

You don't need a total life overhaul to walk in worth. You need a shift.

- From comparison to conviction. Stop measuring your worth against others. Your design is your destiny.

- From hustle to harmony. Worthy people don't run on empty; they operate from overflow.

- From insecurity to identity. The enemy whispers, "Who do you think you are?" God shouts back, "Child of the King."

One adjustment: believe that nothing on earth—no title, no bank statement, no rejection—can change the fact that God has already stamped priceless across your life.

The Story of the Failed Salesman

A man once failed at every sales job he tried. He could never close the deal. Finally, a mentor told him: "The problem is not your pitch. The problem is you don't believe you're worth what you're selling."

That day, he decided to shift his worth. Within months, he became the top salesman, not because he learned new tricks, but because he embraced new truth. That person, my friend, was me.

Learn my Lesson: People don't buy your product first; they buy your confidence. Confidence is the child of self-worth.

Destroying the Drainers of Worth

There are assassins that come for your worth. Let me expose them:

> 1. Comparison. Looking sideways always devalues what's in your hands.
>
> 2. Rejection. People's no does not erase God's yes.
>
> 3. Failure. Falling is an event, not an identity.
>
> 4. Shame. Shame is the graveyard of worth. But Romans 8:1 says, "There is therefore now no condemnation to them which are in Christ Jesus."

These assassins must be executed daily by the Word of God.

Explosive Truth: You Are Not Useless

Let me thunder this in your spirit: You are not useless. You are not hopeless. You are not helpless. The very breath of God in your lungs is proof that you are necessary. Nations may wait on your voice, families on your decisions, industries on your ideas.

The devil doesn't attack trash—he attacks treasure. The storm you're facing is not proof of weakness; it's confirmation of worth.

NET WORTH IS THE FRUIT/ SELF-WORTH IS THE ROOT

Think of a tree. Net worth is the fruit: money, opportunities, influence. Self-worth is the root: unseen, underground, but vital. If the root is diseased, the fruit will be sparse. But when the root is nourished by God's Word, the fruit becomes abundant. Jesus said, "I am come that they might have life, and that they might have it more abundantly" (John 10:10).

Abundance is not measured by the size of your bank account, but by the revelation of who you are in God. Jesus commanded us to love God fully and to love our neighbor as ourselves—which means love for others flows from the value you place on yourself. Romans 12:3 reminds us not to think more highly than we ought, but it never forbids thinking highly of ourselves. To see yourself as worthless is not humility—it is a lie against the God who made you.

Rejection, abandonment, betrayal, even the scars of abuse—these do not define your value. They are events, not identities. Self-worth cannot be stolen by sin, shattered by trauma, or diminished by failure. Why? Because worth was assigned before the wound. The cross is proof: heaven would bankrupt itself just to redeem you.

Hear this: "You are bought with a price" (1 Corinthians 6:20). That price was not silver, not gold, but the blood of Christ. That alone shatters every false narrative.

History is filled with survivors who rose from ashes to influence because they refused to apologize for being chosen. So must you. You are not what happened to you. You are not what was taken from you. You are God's masterpiece. Stand, heal, rise—because your worth has never changed.

Practical Steps to Raise Your Self-Worth

1. Affirm daily: Speak who you are in Christ, not who life tried to label you.

2. Rehearse victories: Stop replaying failures. Even David rehearsed past lion and bear victories before facing Goliath.

3. Invest in yourself: Books, mentors, health—because self-worth grows when you sow into you.

4. Refuse discounting: Don't discount your services, your gifts, or your calling. What God made valuable, don't sell cheap.

5. Worship through worth: Worship isn't groveling; it's agreement with heaven's valuation of you.

The greatest wealth stories are not born in comfort but in conflict. Look at Joseph—betrayed by his brothers, falsely accused, and thrown in prison. Every label shouted "slave, criminal, reject." Yet he chose to see himself as God's dreamer, and that mindset lifted him to second in command over Egypt.

Think of Frederick Douglass, born into slavery, told he was property, yet he refused that label. His self-worth pushed him to literacy, leadership, and influence, shaping nations. Madam C.J. Walker, once a poor washerwoman, endured ridicule for her skin and gender, yet she saw value in herself and became America's first female self-made millionaire.

Steve Jobs, adopted, rejected, and even ousted from the very company he created, believed in his ideas enough to return and revolutionize technology.

Oprah Winfrey, abused and shamed in her youth, was told her voice would never matter. She believed otherwise and built a global media empire.

Andrew Carnegie, a poor Scottish immigrant mocked for his background, chose to think beyond factory work and became one of history's wealthiest men.

Let's broaden the picture. Abraham Lincoln was called unfit for leadership after multiple election defeats and business failures. He pressed forward and became one of the most respected presidents in history.

Thomas Edison was labeled "too stupid to learn" by teachers, yet his belief in his own worth produced over a thousand inventions, including the lightbulb.

The truth remains: rejection cannot bury worth. Each of these lives shows that when self-worth is honored, net worth multiplies. Each of these lives proves a law: self-worth precedes net worth.

They did not wait for validation; they carried it. When they refused to think less of themselves, heaven and earth responded, multiplying their wealth and amplifying their influence.

They believed what God whispered louder than what critics screamed. That unshakable sense of worth transformed them into innovators, leaders, and builders of empires. Their stories prove this eternal truth: self-worth redefined by God becomes net worth magnified by life.

A housewife is not "just at home"—she is a manager of destiny, shaping generations with wisdom. A janitor is not "just cleaning floors"—he is a guardian of health and order, making way for others to thrive. The cashier, the bus driver, the factory worker, the nurse's aide, the delivery driver—each role holds undeniable value. But hear this: the job is never greater than the person. Titles can change, tasks can shift, but your worth is untouchable because it comes from God. When you see yourself as priceless, you elevate how you think, act, and believe—and that shift can multiply your net worth, no matter the position.

A Final Story: The Broken Violin

An auctioneer once held up a battered old violin. He started the bidding at $10. No one wanted it. Then, a master violinist stepped forward, tuned it, and played a melody so rich that the crowd gasped. The bidding soared to thousands.

The violin's worth had not changed—only the revelation of its sound. So it is with you. The Master's hand reveals your value. Your scars, dents, and years of silence cannot diminish your worth. Your net worth is not just about money—it's about influence, relationships, and impact. And it will always mirror your self-worth.

So today, make this decree:

"I am not my performance. I am not my past. I am not my pain. I am worth everything heaven paid for me. I am priceless. I am abundant. I am chosen. I am wealthy in worth, and my life will show it."

About The Author

DR. MIKEL BROWN is an author, businessperson, restaurateur, and religious leader who resides in El Paso, Texas. He is a Licensed Professional Counselor with more than 40 years of experience. He has helped many people achieve success in business, marriage, personal development and peak performance.

Dr. Brown has helped people from rocky marriages to rocketing careers. His private client protégés list range from active and retired professional sports personalities to more than a hundred small business owners. He has over 14 books published, such as *When Lambs Turns Into Lions, Dream Big Start Small, Turn on Your Life, Unexpected Treasures, How to Fix Your Marriage without Using a Hammer,* and *Building Wealth from the Ground Up.*

THE POCKET MOTIVATOR BOOK SERIES

DR. MIKEL A. BROWN

Now You Can Take The Wisdom of Dr. Brown With You Wherever You Go!

GET YOUR COPIES
TODAY!

www.MikelBrown.com

www.ingramcontent.com/pod-product-compliance
Lightning Source LLC
Chambersburg PA
CBHW061806070526
44586CB00023B/2729